Growing a Pizza Garden

BY MADDIE SPALDING

The Child's World®
childsworld.com

Published by The Child's World®
1980 Lookout Drive • Mankato, MN 56003-1705
800-599-READ • www.childsworld.com

Photographs ©: iStockphoto, cover, 1, 5, 6–7, 8,
16–17, 18–19, 20; Marina Lohrbach/Shutterstock
Images, 11; F Delvental CC2.0, 12; Gorilla Images/
Shutterstock Images, 15; Red Line Editorial, 22

ISBN 9781503823792
LCCN 2017944874

Printed in the United States of America
PA02358

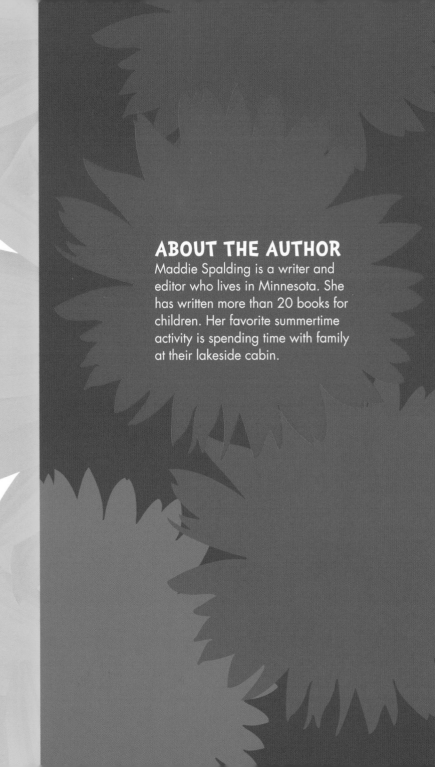

ABOUT THE AUTHOR

Maddie Spalding is a writer and
editor who lives in Minnesota. She
has written more than 20 books for
children. Her favorite summertime
activity is spending time with family
at their lakeside cabin.

Contents

A Sunny Day

It is a sunny summer day! We will grow a pizza garden.

Some people grow vegetables. What vegetables do you like on pizza?

8

First Steps

First we find a sunny spot.

Plants need sun to grow.

Next we lay down **compost**. Compost helps plants grow.

The PIZZA Garden

Wheat & Corn

Fallow :zzzz:

Fallow

Grains of wheat, corn, rye, barley ground into Flour

Tomato Sauce

Tomatoes

Onions & Garlic

Fallow

Fallow (resting...)

Top View

Herbs

Peppers

Hot

Jalapeño

Green Bell Red

Oregano

Cumin Basil

12

The garden is shaped like a circle. Each plant gets its own **section**.

Planting

Other people plant tomatoes. They will grow to be red and juicy. They will taste great on pizza!

We plant peppers. Peppers make pizza colorful!

We plant basil.

Basil is an **herb**.

It is time to water the plants. They take a few weeks to grow. Then they are put on pizza. Yum!

Plant Markers

Use popsicle sticks to make your own plant markers!

Supplies:

1 popsicle stick for each plant
1 paint set with white paint
1 black permanent marker
1 set of colored markers

Instructions:

1. Count the number of plants in your garden.
   You will need 1 popsicle stick for each plant.

2. Paint each stick white. Let the paint dry.

3. Using the marker, label each stick with the name of a plant.

4. Decorate your popsicle sticks using colored markers. Then put
   each stick in your pizza garden.

Glossary

compost — (KOM-post) Compost is a mix of dead leaves and other materials that helps plants to grow. We put compost in our garden.

herb — (URB) An herb is a type of plant that adds flavor to foods. We make our pizza tasty by adding an herb, such as basil.

section — (SEK-shun) A section is a part of an area. Each plant in our pizza garden has its own section.

To Learn More

Books

Amoroso, Cynthia. *Summer*. Mankato, MN: The Child's World, 2014.

Heos, Bridget. *So You Want to Grow a Pizza?* Mankato, MN: Amicus, 2016.

Pierce, Terry. *My Busy Green Garden*. Thomaston, ME: Tilbury House, 2017.

Web Sites

Visit our Web site for links about pizza gardens:
childsworld.com/links

Note to Parents, Teachers, and Librarians: We routinely verify our Web links to make sure they are safe and active sites. So encourage your readers to check them out!

Index